PASSIVE INCOME

Great Tips On How To Make A Passive Income With Great Profits.

Copyright © 2017 Publishing. All Rights Reserved.

No part of this publication may be reproduced, distributed, or transmitted in any form or by any means, including photocopying, recording, or other electronic or mechanical methods, or by any information storage and retrieval system without the prior written permission of the publisher, except in the case of very brief quotations embodied in critical reviews and certain other noncommercial uses permitted by copyright law.

WHY YOU SHOULD READ THIS BOOK

This book will help you know that….

Passive income is what a lot of people think of as "living the dream". If you're earning a passive income, that means that you're making money from a website, a digital product or an affiliate product that you previously set-up. Now you can sit back and relax while the money comes pouring in! Potentially you can scale this business to become very wealthy but either way, you get to benefit from no longer trading your time for money!

But is it really like that? Are you really heading for a lifetime of making money while you relax on beautiful yachts?

TABLE OF CONTENTS

Why You Should Read This Book..iii

Chapter 1: Introduction 1

Chapter 2: Creating Passive Income 3

Chapter 3: Power In Passive Income 10

Chapter 4: Why Only Few Of The Population Is Rich 19

Chapter 5: Proven Business Model And Implementation Method..... 24

Chapter 6: Cost-Effective Marketing Tips That Will Get Your Business Noticed And Earning.. 28

Chapter 7: Tips For Starting A Profitable Company......................... 49

Chapter 8: Conclusion 55

One Last Thing.. 56

Chapter 1
INTRODUCTION

This is Not a Get a Rich Quick Scheme!

Maybe. But the first thing to acknowledge is that this is in no way a "get rich quick" scheme. This is not a method you can use to make money without putting in the equivalent amount of work and time up-front. You are still working for your income; the only difference is that you've done this work up-front as it were.

The other thing to recognize is that this takes a lot of time and a lot of trial and error. In the vast majority of cases, you should not expect to be making hundreds of dollars a day for a long time to come.

Instead, it will take time, work and a lot of patience to eventually get to that point. If you start your passive income business model thinking that you'll be able to quit your day job right away, then you should expect to be very disappointed.

Instead, the best way to think about passive income is a good way to add a little bit of extra revenue to your existing setup. Try to think of eBook sales or clicks on adverts as extra income and as a way to improve your overall salary.

This way, you won't be disappointed even if you're only making $20 in eBook sales a week. That's still $80 a month and $960 a year... enough to go on a good holiday!

But more importantly, once you start making this money and you enjoy making that much, you'll find that it starts to increase. If you don't get quickly frustrated and give up on your passive businesses, then they will grow over time and start to make more and more money.

That's how you successfully grow your passive income and it's what will eventually allow you to give up your day job.

Endless Scalability

The other great thing about passive income models is that they are endlessly scalable. Because you aren't trading man-hours for money, that means there's no limit to how many times you can repeat the same business model over and over again.

Making a profit from selling an eBook on Kindle? Then why not make another? And another? And another? This way, you can multiply your sales over and over again.

And eventually, you're almost sure to land on that "big hit" that will be your real cash cow. It takes time, it takes patience and it takes luck. But it's worth it!

CHAPTER 2
CREATING PASSIVE INCOME

There are a number of ways which can help you generate wealth. Some of the ways requires that you work extra hard while others just need good brains that can help you generate of passive income. Number of tips that can be handy and which may help you make money.

Let's face it, nobody likes the idea of a late night phone call from a bad tenant complaining about a leaking toilet or busted pipe. I can tell you first hand that it certainly isn't what you want to experience on a Friday night. For many people, being a hands-on landlord just doesn't fit with their desired lifestyle. And while the benefits of owning rental properties are tremendous, that is certainly understandable.

Is there a way to generate substantial passive income using real estate without these late night phone calls and the headaches of dealing with less than desirable tenants?

What is truly amazing about real estate investing is there is absolutely no need to try and fit a square peg in a round hole. There are many different ways other than owning rental properties to generate significant passive income while still being secured by a hard asset. One of my favorite investment strategies that I have utilized extensively over the years is owner financing.

In this book we will look at the benefits of owner financing and see if this could be a good fit for your financial and life style goals.

How To Develop Passive Income Streams:

Are you interested in developing a passive income stream to supplement your lifestyle? There are many opportunities to earn a lucrative passive income stream, this is a list of seven that you can use to boost your income. These are available for any aspiring entrepreneur. Included with each income opportunity is a brief overview, giving you a better understanding of what will work for you in your situation. You can utilize one, two or more of these income generating opportunities. So let's get started.

- **Blogging**

Blogging has taken the online world by storm and anyone has the opportunity to be a publisher on this platform. It's possible to publish a blog on any content that you can think of. Here are some figures from WordPress.com:

- 77 million Word Press sites worldwide
- 13.1 billion blog pages
- 409 million monthly readers
- 38.7 million new post each month
- 50 million comments monthly

With numbers like this you can see how a blog site can launch you to phenomenal success. Giving you the opportunity to launch all your passive income streams from one hub. A blog gives you the opportunity to brand yourself and develop an online presence; it's your gateway for driving targeted traffic to your online passive income opportunities.

- **Internet Publisher**

In 2015 approximately $135 billion were invested by business owners and marketing teams to create new digital marketing platforms to promote their brands, products or services. One media source reported that 25% of all the advertising market was using this platform. 73% of businesses polled planned on increasing their advertising budget for Google Ad Words.

Different advertising platforms are:

- Google ad words 73%
- Bing ads 55%
- display networks 52%
- Facebook 52%
- LinkedIn 26%
- Twitter 24%
- smaller social networks 18%

By becoming a publisher on these platforms you can earn a lucrative passive income. By getting targeted prospects to click and take action on the ads posted on websites, blogs, review sites, landing pages, splash pages and other online channels you can generate a sizable passive income stream. The more traffic you target will generate a higher potential for getting better click-through with your ads. Helping you to sell any kind of product or service generating passive income for you. With this type of advertising it's imperative that you develop targeted advertising skills for keywords in the niche that you're trying to work with.

- **Affiliate Marketing**

Last year $14.94 billion were registered in the affiliate marketing industry, showing that this is a very lucrative source for passive income. By using affiliate networks like Click Bank, Click promise, Commission junction or other affiliate marketing sources you will be able to earn commissions anywhere from 5% to as much as 90% selling other people's products. Also you have the ability to generate even more revenue by creating and marketing your own products through these affiliate networks. The most important factor to success is driving highly targeted audience to your affiliate landing pages or sales pages that you have registered with. And this should always be done with your own targeted funnel system beginning with landing pages you've designed to collect data before sending prospects to the affiliate landing page. Or you can use other digital marketing tools to drive traffic to your affiliate link utilizing blogging or social media like Facebook or Twitter.

- **Amazon**

These days Amazon e-books have outpaced traditional publishing company and account for up to 20% of the total Internet traffic. As an Amazon associate you can leverage on this traffic and earn passive income. If you have a website or a blog that talks about a certain product or category niche you can earn from the volume based fixed advertising rates Amazon Associates offer for products sold through a certain category. Working with Amazon is a fairly simple process and they will help you set up your business through their system.

- **Freelancing**

Another way to earn a lucrative income online is by providing freelancing services today there is an estimated 20% to 33% volume of independent workers out of the total size of the workforce in the United States. And organizations are planning to increase their dependence on freelancers, last year alone there was almost a 50% increase in freelancers hired. And the pay is getting better for freelancers as well, increasing by 37% year on year. There is a wide variety of skills and expertise needed for freelancers. Some of the highest rated skills that are being outsourced by employers to freelancers today are:

- IT and programming
- design and multimedia
- writing in translation
- and smaller niche markets

So if you're interested in freelancing this could be a lucrative passive income stream for you.

- **Online Content Writer**

These days as the search engine algorithms move towards more focused, high quality and well written original content, the demand for online writers has been increasing making it a very lucrative source of online income. The average hourly rate for an online writer is approximately $27 an hour which is much better than the federal minimum wage.

50% of the B2B marketers plan on increasing in the next 12 months, their content marketing budgets and as much as 40% of these companies outsource their B2B content generation activities to freelance online writers. This gives you an excellent opportunity to develop a passive online income stream to supplement your finances.

- **Network Marketing**

Network marketing or MLM is basically a form of direct selling and is also known as person to person marketing. In network marketing you earn by directly selling products to other customers. You can also earn a passive income stream by building your own network of independent distributors otherwise known as your "network" giving you the ability to earn from different levels of residual income from their sales and memberships.

In the last few years network marketing has grown substantially and has become the source of income for many successful network marketers, as many as 150,000 people signed up in these networking systems on a daily basis. There is over 50 million people worldwide who have joined network marketing companies, reaching a worldwide sales as high as $90 billion. These days many people utilize the Internet, to develop their network by developing blogs and landing pages to sign up new recruits and to harvest email information to market to later. This can be developed into a very profitable income stream possibly giving you the opportunity to finance your total lifestyle instead of supplementing a traditional job.

As an experienced blogger and network marketer I know it's difficult to find training, if you would like to have a 14 day 100% FREE training course that would teach you how to develop your own online network marketing business with a funnel system that attracts high converting leads then go to create my Breakthrough.

Chapter 3
Power in Passive Income

Time is precious. It's sacred. Just 24 hours in a day. That's all we get. Not one person on this earth has more time than that. No matter their age, occupation, religion, color of their skin or where they live. No one time is the greatest equalizer because not a single person can have more of it. It can never be recreated or re-spent. It exists once, and then it's gone. And that's precisely why passive income is so important because time is more valuable than money.

Unlike money, which can be earned, saved, spent, invested, squandered and lost, we can't tuck away minutes on a clock. We can't expect dividends on seconds or hours in the bank, or invest the time that we didn't use on something else. Considering that most of the free world needs to work for a living, consuming much of the time they do have, this precious commodity needs to be nurtured and savored.

Passive income is quite possibly one of the most important and central ways that the rich get richer. It's how you detach your ability to earn from the time that you do have in a day. If you've ever heard the term, making money while you sleep, no truer words have been spoken. With passive income, you do make money while you sleep. You also make money while you're awake. It's automatic and simply keeps coming in.

However, creating a passive income stream is far from automatic. It's no easy feat by any measure. It takes an enormous amount of effort and exertion of your time with very little return in the beginning. It involves an overall sense of frustration and an enormous learning curve. Still, it's one of the most fruitful and worthwhile investments of your time that you could possibly engage in.

While passive income might not be the answer to all of your immediate problems, it is the pathway to success and most certainly the foundation for wealth and happiness. When you're not stressed just to make enough money to pay the bills and you're no longer living from paycheck-to-paycheck, there's a mental clarity and an emotional catharsis that sets in. You become free from the shackles of a life-sucking 9-to-5 job and begin embracing a more fulfilled life.

When you have the time to choose to work or spend those precious moments with your children or go on some trip halfway around the world, you're free. You're free in the greatest sense of the word. Aren't the entire headache and the hassle worth that? Isn't it time to break the chains that have restrained you to a life that's been less fulfilled? I would think so. And I would imagine that if you truly are serious about getting rich in life, then you'll embrace the passive-income machine.

What Is Passive Income?

Before I dive into the reasons why passive income is so important, let's first describe what it actually is. Passive income is income that's received automatically with little requirement for maintenance. In contrast, active income can only be earned by directly translating your time for money. Whether it's a pay-per-hour job or a salaried one, the amount of money you make is directly correlated to your time.

With active income, when you don't work, you can't earn. If something were to happen to you and you were incapacitated for whatever reason through an injury, illness or some other calamity, you would lose your ability to earn. If, for example, you were an athlete and you injured yourself so badly that you were unable to continue your occupation, you would lose your ability to compete and earn money altogether.

If you work as a contractor or a builder, without mobility and the usage of all your limbs, how could you work? If something were to happen to you and you lost a leg or an arm, how could you continue to earn money? If you got sick and needed an organ transplant and were out of work for months, how long do you think your employer would keep you on before letting you go? If your car broke down and you didn't have money to fix it, how could you go show homes as a realtor or meet with prospective clients in any other capacity? It would certainly become far more difficult.

Most of the world lives in accordance to an active-income credo. They earn only based on the time that they work. The wealthy, however, operate on another set of standards, which involve a detachment of their physical time for the money that they earn. They earn passive income from a number of sources such as real estate rentals, dividends, interest income, royalties, franchise fees, Laundromats, website advertisements and so on.

Now, don't get me wrong. Creating a passive income stream is a massive undertaking. It involves the investment of a tremendous amount of time. During that investment of time, you receive no income. You're investing your time with the hopes of producing an income down the road, not today. With active income, the money you earn is directly correlated to the time you work. But passive income continues to pay you long after the work has been completed.

Clearly, there are a number of ways to make passive income. Whether you're looking to make money online or simply earn passive income through more traditional means such as real estate rentals, there are a number of ways to produce these types of income streams. While difficult at first, what you'll come to realize is not only the importance of having passive income in your life, but you'll also become addicted to it, seeking out ways to produce additional streams of this powerful fiscal method.

So when it comes down to it, there are likely dozens of reasons why having passive income is important in your life. This doesn't mean that you have to quit your active-income employment. Of course, if you can afford to do that and throw yourself at passive-income generation, then you'll fare much better down the road. But many people simply can't afford to do that. With debt and other financial obligations, going without income for a specific period is simply not feasible for most.

The Reasons Why Passive Income Is So Important

- **Passive Income Gives You The Freedom Of Time**

All things considered, time is our greatest asset. In fact, time is far more valuable than money. While money can be spent and earned, time can only be used up but just once. After that time has passed, it's gone forever. You can never physically relive that moment again. This is why passive income is so important because it gives you the freedom of time. When you're less shackled by the necessity to earn just to meet your monthly financial obligations, you have the freedom of time.

This doesn't mean you have total freedom from all of life's obligations; it simply means that you have the flexibility that comes along with not having to struggle to make ends meet at the end of the month. As long as you can ensure that your passive income outpaces your monthly expenses, you're free to spend your time as you choose. With each new passive income stream, your revenue eventually far surpasses your expenses and you ultimately attain true financial freedom.

When you have freedom of time because you're not engaged in active-income work, you're free to do as you please. You can choose to travel the world and become a digital nomad. You can choose to settle down and start a family. You can engage in work related to creating additional passive-income streams of revenue. The choice is yours. You have the freedom to choose because you have the freedom of time. That's the power of passive income.

- **It Reduces Your Stress, Anxiety And Fear Of The Future**

There's nothing worse than having the pressure that comes along with an inability to pay your bills. It causes anxiety, fear and an overall hopeless desperation for the future. The what-if scenarios begin to encircle your mind, like a hawk flying above its prey prior to swooping in for the kill. It does a number on you mentally, physically and spiritually. It emotionally beats you up and destroys your hopes and aspirations.

Anytime we live in dire fear of the future, it's hard to be present. It's hard to enjoy what we have in the here-and-now because we're so tied up with those doomsday scenarios. We're so worried about an impending fiscal collapse that it's hard to extricate ourselves from the shackles of that train of thought. It consumes and becomes you. It's hard to get away from that when it's all you can think about.

Passive income helps to alleviate all of these worries. It helps to put fears to bed because you aren't worried about losing your job or being the byproduct of corporate-downsizing. When you don't have to worry so much about impending financial doom, not only do you feel better mentally and emotionally, but it translates into physical vitality. You have more energy and are more motivated to get out there and achieve more because passive income also helps to build that all-important financial momentum in life.

- **It Allows You To Pursue Doing The Things You Love Rather Than What Pays The Bills**

We all have things that we're passionate about doing in life. But we always seem to put them off for later. Whether it's art or music or travel, we can indulge our fantasies when passive income frees us from debt that tethers us to the never-ending cycle of payments and interest. It allows you to exit that proverbial rat race by elevating you above all the things that worry so-called "normal folks."

It also frees you to produce an active income by following your heart. When your passive income outpaces your debts, why not get involved with a project that you care deeply about? Maybe you want to help out at a homeless shelter downtown that can't pay you. Maybe you want you to teach your neighbor's son piano lessons and they can't pay you much. Whatever it is, you can do it because you're not worried about the paycheck.

It doesn't matter what you're passionate about, you can do it. If you want to take a language class for a few weeks and study full time, you can. When you want to go camping with your kids for a full week, you can. You don't need to worry about calling in sick or taking time off from work. You're your own boss. It's the dream of those out there that wake up every single day dreading another moment of work that totally and utterly bores them.

- **It Gives You The Ability To Live And Work From Anywhere**

I don't know about you, but I have a deep-down passion for travel. If I were to categorize the things in this world that I love the most as a pastime, that would be amongst one of the top contenders. But the problem with travel, for most people, is that it's temporary. It's a momentary state of bliss that seems to come and go too fast. But this isn't about just taking a week-or-two vacation from work; this is about really traveling the world with the ability to work (or not) from any place.

When you have passive income, you can pick up and hit the open road. You can head to a city like Chiang Mai, Bangkok, Berlin, or just about any other place on the planet, live and work. You can exist for peanuts on the dollar compared to most other major metropolises around the planet. But you don't need to stay. You can continue to wander after just a few months. And why not when you have the financial ability to do so?

Still, it's easy to not put passive income as a priority when you're so actively concerned about the day-to-day. Rising above that is difficult. But you just need to set a goal, focus and move towards that goal with persistent action on a daily basis. There is light at the end of the tunnel. It will take you time, but you'll eventually get there. It all just depends on how badly you want it and how important it is to you at the end of the day.

- **It Provides A Platform For Financial Stability And Growth**

When your income is automatic, and you don't need to worry about meeting your expenses at the end of the month by exchanging your direct time for money, it allows you to think and explore new ways to further strengthen your financial stability, and to grow it. It gives you the time to research things like taxes, stocks and other investments. This helps to create fiscal clarity in your mind, fueling you towards your financial goals.

It's easier to train your focus on your finances when you're not pulled in so many other directions. While problems can and still will arise in your life, financially and otherwise, you'll be better prepared to deal with them. Without having the obligation of rushing off to a job you dread every single day, you can train your mind's eye on the things that will provide you with greater growth and prosperity over time. No matter how you look at it, the importance of passive income is paramount. Many people discount it because they either don't understand it or don't think that having passive income that exceeds your expenses isn't an attainable goal. Well, whatever the mind believes, the mind can achieve. That's as true for passive income as it is for anything else in life. Believe it wholeheartedly with your spirit, and you can accomplish it. As long as you don't give up.

CHAPTER 4
WHY ONLY FEW OF THE POPULATION IS RICH

"Why is it that people don't become wealthy?"

In a country like ours, with the opportunities that we have, why is it that so few people retire financially independent? And I eventually found the answers. Here are what I consider to be the five reasons why people don't become wealthy.

Who Am I?

First, at the top of the list, is that it never occurs to them.

The average person has grown up in a family where he has never met or known anyone who was wealthy. He goes to school and socializes with people who are not wealthy. He works with people who are not wealthy. He has a reference group or a social circle outside of work that are not wealthy. He has no role models who are wealthy. If this has happened to you throughout your formative years, up to the age of twenty, you can grow up and become a fully mature adult in our society, and it may never occur to you that it's just as possible for you to become wealthy as for anyone else.

This is why people who grow up in homes where their parents are wealthy are much more likely to become wealthy as adults then people who grew up in homes where their parents are not. So the first reason why people don't become wealthy is it never occurs to them that it is possible for them. And of course, if it never occurs to them, then they never take any of the steps necessary to make it a reality.

- **Make A Decision**

The second reason that people don't become wealthy is that they never decide to.

Even if a person reads a book, attends a lecture, or associates with people who are financially successful, nothing changes until he makes a decision to do something different. Even if it occurs to a person that he could become wealthy if he just did certain things in a specific way, if he doesn't decide to take the first step, he ends up staying as he is.

If you continue to do what you've always done, you'll continue to get what you've always got.

The primary reason for underachievement and failure is that the great majority of people don't decide to be successful. They never make a firm, unequivocal commitment or definite decision that they are going to become wealthy. They mean to, and they intend to, and they hope to and they're going to, someday. They wish and hope and pray that they will make a lot of money, but they never decide, "I am going to do it!" This decision is an essential first step to becoming financially independent.

- **Maybe Tomorrow**

The third reason that people don't become wealthy is procrastination.

People always have a good reason not to begin doing what they know they need to do to achieve financial independence. It is always the wrong month, the wrong season, or the wrong year. Business conditions in their industry are no good, or they may be too good. The market isn't right. They may have to take a risk, or give up their security. Maybe next year. There always seems to be a reason to procrastinate. As a result, they keep putting it off, month by month, year by year, until it's too late. Even if it has occurred to a person that they can become wealthy, and they have made a decision to change, procrastination will push all their plans into the indefinite future.

- **Pay The Price**

The fourth reason that people retire poor is what economists call the inability to delay gratification.

The great majority of people have an irresistible temptation to spend every single penny they make and whatever else they can borrow or buy on credit. If you cannot delay gratification, and discipline yourself to refrain from spending everything you make, you cannot become wealthy. If you cannot practice budgeting as a lifelong habit, it will be impossible for you to achieve financial independence.

As **W. Clement Stone** said, *"If you cannot save money, the seeds of greatness are not in you."*

- **Take The Long View**

The fifth reason that people retire poor is perhaps as important, if not more important, than all the others…

It is lack of time perspective.

In a longitudinal study conducted by Dr. Edward Banfield at Harvard University in the 1950s and published in 1964 as The Unheavenly City, he studied the reasons for upward socio-economic mobility. He wanted to know how you could predict whether an individual or a family was going to move upward one or more socio-economic groupings and be wealthier in the next generation than they were this generation.

All his research brought him to a single factor that he concluded was more accurate than any other in predicting success in America. They called it time perspective. This was defined as the amount of time that you take into consideration when planning your day-to-day activities and when making important decisions in your life. Time perspective referred to how far you projected into the future when you decided what you were going to do or not do in the present.

An example of long time perspective is the common habit of upper class families in England to register their children at Oxford or Cambridge as soon as the child is born, even though he or she will not be attending for eighteen or nineteen years.

This is long time perspective in action. The young couple that begins putting $50 dollars a month aside in a scholarship fund so that their newborn child can go to the college or university of his or her choice is a couple with long time perspective.

They are willing to sacrifice in the short term to assure better results and outcomes in the long term. People with long time perspective almost invariably move up economically in the course of their lifetimes.

Chapter 5
PROVEN BUSINESS MODEL AND IMPLEMENTATION METHOD

When it comes to setting up an internet-based business, identifying the right business model is the key to success. However, results may vary from one person to another due to certain factors. The factors that you should consider when selecting the most appropriate business model include your skills, experience, your personality, your preference, the amount of time and capital you can dedicate towards the business.

The following are the top 10 internet business models. They are proven business models that are winners time and time again.

- **Selling Internet Download Type Products**

Selling products in digital form that are downloadable on the internet is the fastest moving commodity among internet businesses. The product could be eBooks, software, music, movies, photos and computer games. As the entrepreneur, you may be the one that creates the product or you could buy the product and sell on at a profit. You may sell the product yourself or collaborate with resellers to increase your distribution channels. This type of business model has low capital outlay, high profit margins and works best when you can sell the product in volumes. Overheads in this top 10 internet business model are minimal as the process of product delivery fully automated.

PROVEN BUSINESS MODEL AND IMPLEMENTATION METHOD

- **Affiliate Marketing**

In this model, you market the goods and services of another person. It is similar to multilevel marketing for non-internet based businesses. To set up this internet business model, you will need to first own a website. You then create links from your website to the website of the business whose product you are marketing. You receive payment when a visitor to your website clicks and buys a product the website you are promoting. Third party websites such as ClickBank.com handles the payment process to make ensure you are paid.

- **Ad sense Model**

Ad sense model among the clearly proven business models because it is one of Google's primary sources of income. All you do is register for the service and then have Google strategically position Google advertisements on you web pages. Google will pay you each time someone clicks on an advert on your website. For best results, you have to grow the user traffic to your website using various search engine optimization techniques.

- **Click per action (CPA Model)**

Click per action (CPA) business model is a deviation from affiliate marketing. You get payment when leads from your website go to another website -and they take a specific action on the final website. The person may only be required to join an email list, subscribe to a free newsletter or join a free e-learning training module. The key to success here is you and the advertisers have agreed on payment and terms...hence the name cost per action. This is a recent top internet business model that is growing in popularity because it is easier to get your prospects to subscribe to a free service than it is to make them buy a product.

- **Membership Model**

This proven business model involves having visitors to your website pay a regular fee in order to access the information or services you have available. This is a popular model with many of the larger internet businesses such as websites of mainstream newspapers, magazines and professional associations. The greatest benefit of this model is you have consistent income streams.

- **Building an Email List**

Here you get as many people as you can to sign up to your mailing list after which you regularly send them information on a given niche. You can then add affiliate links and CPA advertisements to boost your income. In this business model, only send to people that subscribe for your service because you may run the risk of spamming emails and blacklisting by internet service providers.

- **Niche Content Websites**

Niche content websites are websites built around providing authoritative information on a given subject matter. Traffic to your site will continue to grow as more people consider your website a leader in your field. You can then use your website's visibility to market your products while you provide good quality content-that attracted visitors to your website in the first place.

PROVEN BUSINESS MODEL AND IMPLEMENTATION METHOD

Your prospects are more responsive to your sales message-because they trust you.

- **Blogging Model**

Blogging operates similarly to the niche content website in that you take one subject and focus your blog on that one area. The main difference is that a blog is often more interactive than the niche content website even though you can have a blog within your website.

- **Internet Services Model**

This is one of the oldest models and even though it's a saturated market segment, it is one of the proven business models. Here, you sell various internet related services such as web hosting, SEO services and other e-commerce solutions.

- **E Coaching Model**

E coaching and E-training is a fast growing top 10-internet business model. In this model, you provide paying clients coaching in the field of your expertise. You can charge a monthly rate or per training module. The main attraction for prospects is the cost benefit-because a typical coaching module offline could be double the cost delivered online. The key to success is to get effective and low cost platforms for delivering your training modules. You can leverage these proven models to succeed online. Choose one and start taking action. It's about ready, fire aim.

Chapter 6
Cost-Effective Marketing Tips That Will Get Your Business Noticed and Earning

If you want to get into network marketing but aren't sure how then you're in the right place. With the information in this book you should start to build your knowledge about network marketing and from there formulate your own strategies for success. If you do all that then you should be well on your way.

Keep your positivity high when starting out in network marketing. It is much harder to stay positive than it is to be negative, however, it is important to your success. If you are getting stressed out, imagine the revenue that you will be generating when you are a success. Believe it or not, you will get through these early days.

Approach people with questions, not statements. If you give someone the opportunity to answer a question, you are starting a conversation. Approaching with a statement doesn't give the prospect an opening to interact with you and can be a real turn off. When someone gets to answer a question they feel involved in the process and are more attuned to listening to you.

Pay yourself first in your network marketing business. This is the most important thing to keep in mind in any business, but with network marketing strategies it tends to be overlooked often. You can put some money back into the business as necessary, but make sure that your account keeps track of that fact so you can be paid back at a later time.

When speaking to a possible recruit, in person or electronically, learn all you can about their life and then tailor your marketing towards how your business can better their life. Many people love the idea of working from home during hours they set themselves, so that is a great way to slant your sales pitch.

In network marketing success it is critical that you never give up. You need to make a commitment to be working one year from today. Do not give up after a few months because you ran into problems or encountered some obstacles. You have to be persistent and keep putting one foot in front of the other to achieve success.

Managing your time wisely is critical to the success of your network marketing business. While reading blogs about internet marketing is interesting, you could have used that time to promote your own product with your own blog. Be persistent in calling your down-lines to get them motivated, but cut your losses if they haven't responded by the fourth call, and put your energy to use in more productive endeavors. Training calls and conferences are great, but they don't create prospects for you. Neither does training agents for other team members. Avoid companies with an all-for-one, one-for-all attitude. You're in business to make money for yourself, not other network marketers.

Content marketing – Learn how to use content to market your business!

Content marketing works. In fact, so long as the material you produce is of extremely good quality, Content Marketing can work REALLY well. Last year, I generated over £150,000 in fees and sales from this blog, exclusively through Content Marketing. You may or may not be familiar with the phrase Content Marketing, yet you visit content marketing sites every time you access the Internet. When you visit news sites, entertainment sites or blogs like this, which offer business advice, you are visiting a site that uses content (useful information) to market itself. Content Marketing can successfully be used to market any type of business and it is unbeatable when it comes to attracting new clients, sales leads, inquiries and subscribers.

Briefly, here's how Content Marketing works:

You create a website, blog, newsletter or podcast, etc. You use it to provide FREE information that has real value to your prospective clients, whilst offering them the opportunity to purchase goods, services (or both), which are closely linked to the information you give away.

For instance, on this blog I provide thousands of marketing ideas and regular, valuable, free marketing advice. People read the information, use the ideas and share what they find here with their friends. Then, some of those people see the quality of my information and decide to hire me, when they need expert marketing help. Others buy my audio program.

Email marketing – Start using email marketing NOW!

Email marketing is extremely cost effective and one of the most powerful marketing tools available to small businesses. This is because it provides predictable results and costs little or nothing to use Business owners who spent time and money building their Facebook Page discovered in 2013, that Facebook is showing their posts to just a tiny fraction of their fans. If they want all their Facebook fans to see their posts, they now need to pay Facebook. Facebook owns their network! This change of the rules is a perfect example of why you need to avoid outsourcing your network, to a social network. Email marketing puts you in control and allows you to build an increasingly valuable asset.

Here are just a few things for you to consider, before you start using email marketing.

I strongly recommend that you build your own email database, rather than buy one from one of those list broking companies.

The best way to start building your subscriber list, is to ask all your existing clients and contacts if you can have their email address. Never just add people to your email list. You need permission; otherwise they will regard your emails as spam.

Then, ask if you can contact them from time to time via email with a newsletter or special offers or announcements. This will get you your initial list and give you something to get started with. So long as you ONLY contact these people with useful information, and make it easy for them to share your newsletter, your list will grow… in size and value.

You also need to have an email sign-up box on your website or blog. This needs to be easy to read and positioned in an uncluttered area of your site, which everyone will see. I offer a free email version of this blog. The subscriber box is clearly positioned on the top right of the site. This position works extremely well and people use it every hour of every day to subscribe.

Be extremely cautious of any marketing expert, who says you need to use annoying pop-up boxes in order to get their reader's attention. **NO YOU DO NOT**. It simply shows they have no idea how to optimize their website.

Build a well-connected network

One of the biggest myths in business is that you must have a large network if you want to succeed. In fact, you need just 5 or 10 people to begin with.

The reality is that the size of your network is not what's important. It's the influence of the people within your network that counts.

IF MY NETWORK has 1000 people BUT they lack influence, it will have a commercial value of close to zero.

IF YOUR NETWORK has just 10 people BUT they are motivated and have real influence, it will have a massive commercial value to you.

(Tip: I explain this in more detail here).

Stop wasting your time swapping business cards at networking events. The people attending these events are there to sell to you, not to buy from you and very, very few well-connected people waste their time attending them. None of the influential people I know or have met over my 25 years in marketing, network at these events. The best networkers have discovered out that the way to get connected to the right people is to deliberately target them.

Here's a suggestion: Draw up a list of the 30 most influential people in your marketplace. These people could include high quality prospective clients or maybe influential introducers; introducers are people who can recommend you to lots of buyers. Then, put a plan together that will allow you to EARN their attention. This targeted approach takes time, but the rewards are enormous. Don't believe me? Okay, think how different your business would look, if you had already done this, and you could now pick up the phone and talk to the most influential people in your industry! It's a game-changer.

Hopefully with the information you learned in this book you have the knowledge you need to get started in it. Remember that the information in this article is only a portion of what you can know, if you keep on expanding your knowledge then success with network marketing should come in no time.

Detailed, real-world information to help you define strategies, costs and benefits for each online business.

Benefit Of Blogging For Online Business

I'm often asked whether blogging is really a necessary part of running a business. This question is most often asked by small business owners who simply don't have the time or skills to regularly create high-quality content. And even if they did? They wouldn't have a clue what to write about. As a business owner who has built a successful business in large part thanks to blogging and content publication, I've seen firsthand the difference it can make in terms of search visibility, leads, and sales. I'm a huge advocate of investing heavily in a content publication strategy, and that strategy begins with the company blog.

- **Increases Search Engine Traffic**

In terms of search engine rankings, I like to think of blogging as fishing. The more hooks you have in the water, the more likely you are to catch a fish. In the same way, as you add more content to your site, more pages from your domain become indexed in search engines. This improves organic search visibility and increases website traffic. Every new page you publish is like dropping another hook in the water. With more opportunities for your target market to find your bait, the more bites you'll get. The more blog posts you have, the more chances you have to rank for various keywords.

- **Humanizes Your Brand**

Carefully crafted website content (e.g., a homepage or about page) can't hold a candle to a blog post when it comes to showing the personal side of your business. Blogging gives your business a way to touch on issues and concerns of interest to your prospects, while also sharing what you and your employees are passionate about. Your blog posts give you a unique opportunity to share your voice and personality, building up trust and increasing your brand's likeability quotient.

- **Supports Your Social Media Initiatives**

It's difficult to maintain an active social media presence without access to unique, high-quality content. Sharing other people's content on social media is great, but at some point you want to be directing those leads to your own site. As you share your blog posts on social media, you increase traffic to your business website - a feat that would be much more difficult without highly-relevant, topical information such as that found in blog posts.

In addition, blog posts provide content for email newsletters. If you've got an email newsletter, you've probably wondered what content should go in it. A simple top-10 list that highlights your best blog content over the last 2-4 weeks is valuable content that's likely to be appreciated by your readers.

- **Builds Authority In Your Industry**

A blog is one of the best ways to establish yourself or your brand as an expert in your field, as it gives you a platform for sharing important industry-related information and insights. As you build up authority in your niche, this breeds trust and familiarity, keeping you top-of-mind when your prospects are ready to buy, and increasing conversion rates, which brings us to our next benefit...

- **Helps you rank for long-tail search queries**

A site without a blog will have a hard time ranking for long-tail search queries. A typical business website can often successfully rank for business-specific keywords (e.g., "Joe's Drycleaners"), but will have a more difficult time ranking for highly-specific phrases like "How to get red wine out of silk". Having more content is the best way to rank for long-tail queries; the more content you add, the more chances you have to rank for less common, but ultimately higher-converting keyword phrases.

Benefits Of Online Advertising

- **Cost efficiency:** Your online ads will be viewed by millions of people, 24 hours a day. You can't say that about print advertising or direct mail. Plus, when you have your own Portal, consider cooperative advertising efforts such as banner swaps. You can't get much more cost-effective than free!

Social media, of course, can also be free via posts and Tweets. And pay-per-impression or pay-per-click advertising allows you to pay only when your ad is seen or clicked on. The beauty of the web is that hosts like Google can deliver your ads directly to people who are interested in your products, delivering far more bang for your buck than other types of advertising.

- **Native Advertising/Advertorials:** Advertorials, also known as native advertising, were once anathema to print publishers. But today, with greater care taken to produce truly relevant and valuable content, and to mark the advertorial as exactly what it is, advertorials are becoming much more widely accepted on the Internet.

The best advertorials showcase the advertiser's expertise without being blatantly promotional. Check out all the different types of native ads, and then a few native advertising examples who are knocking it out of the park.

Benefits of Affiliate Marketing

If you've been in the ecommerce space for a little while, you're most likely familiar with the term "affiliate marketing." But many people aren't quite sure what it actually is or how the process works. In its simplest terms, affiliate marketing is a performance-based marketing model that rewards affiliate partners for driving a desired action. These actions can include site visits, completion of a lead form and/or converted sales. This form of marketing can be an incredibly beneficial, low-risk way to promote your products.

To help you understand the real benefits of affiliate marketing, we've created a list of what we consider the top 5 benefits of affiliate marketing:

- **Performance-Based**

The main advantage of having an affiliate program is that it is entirely performance-based. Because affiliates are only paid a commission once the desired action has taken place, they're more motivated to drive the conversion you're looking for. This mitigates any efforts that drive traffic with little to no value to your company while also ensuring that you get what you pay for.

- **Broader Marketing Efforts**

Affiliates can be found in every market and product category that exists today. Whether you're looking to break into the retail industry or for something more niche like handcrafted vintage toys, there will always be relevant websites to align with. The great news is that many of these affiliates will already have an established visitor base. These partnerships grant the opportunity to expand out into new markets that you might not otherwise have had the bandwidth to explore or to further saturate your existing target markets, giving your brand a much stronger online presence. Think of these partners as an extension of your current marketing or sales team.

- **3rd Party Validation**

By partnering with trusted bloggers and reputable websites, you can further the reputation of your brand and its products. These partners will champion your products and, in our opinion, will further solidify consumer confidence in your product or service. While in the research phase of a purchase, consumers are more likely to trust a 3rd party's opinion over content produced directly from the site selling this product. Consumers also have a certain level of trust in websites they frequent for product recommendations.

- **Cost Effective**

For many of the reasons listed above, affiliate marketing can be extremely cost effective. If you're only paying commissions when the desired conversion occurs, you're not throwing away ad dollars on placements that have no proven value. Furthermore, recruiting affiliates in new markets is an easy way to branch out into that market without the overhead cost of creating an entire marketing campaign, mitigating the need to sink money into an unproven market for testing.

- **Rapidly Scale Traffic**

In conjunction with your other marketing efforts, recruiting affiliates to your program will allow you to scale traffic faster. The more sites that link to your pages, the more opportunities you'll have to convert those users into paid customers. The other benefit of having these sites link back to yours is the added value search engines will put on your site. Essentially having outside resources link back to your site positively effects your search engine ranking, which will compliment your existing SEO efforts.

Affiliate marketing can be a very effective, low-risk investment to help expand your marketing efforts beyond a small business' traditional bandwidth. For the reasons listed here, we believe affiliate marketing is worth the investment and can take your program to new heights.

Benefits of Selling on Amazon

- **Amazon Has The Numbers**

This is not intended to be a mean question at all, but if you polled 100 people in the street, would they be likelier to have heard of your store or Amazon? Amazon and other giant online marketplaces have a cachet to their names because of how big they are and how long they've been around.

Also, because you haven't publicly earned your stripes the way big-name online marketplaces have, customers are less likely to trust you. This in no way means you're a bad online retailer, only that you'd have a lot more work on your hands establishing that trust with your own site than if you went with an existing marketplace.

Infrastructure That's Hard to Compete With As a disclaimer, we're not telling you to abandon your site completely. After all, if everyone with a genius idea did that, we'd never have the likes of Facebook, Amazon or Google. But keep in mind that you're going head-to-head with really big players, the likes of whom have invested billions of dollars in infrastructure and technology to create an amazing buying experience regardless of platform.

Money can achieve a lot in the online world. Having a fat wallet may not automatically guarantee a spot in the top three, but it can buy the things, ideas and people that make it possible. And Amazon has continually used its money to build out an ecosystem that would be almost impossible for a new seller to replicate in any way—its scale allows for super-competitive pricing and its structure and business model ensures millions of active third party sellers choose it as their primary online sales channel.

Fees or Large Overheads?

We often hear about the fees Amazon charges, and how they can eat into profits, but looking solely at the fees is a huge mistake. Remarkably, the online sellers who choose to build their own online store as their primary sales channel to avoid continuing fees, simply ignore or underestimate the huge overhead in time and money of both building an ecommerce store and of driving traffic to it (on an on-going business)—not to mention the risk involved in pouring a large sum of money into a venture that has no guaranteed success. Amazon's route allows you to start selling online with little risk and most of its fees are only incurred upon selling, so they're predetermined and easily accounted for in your pricing structure.

Customers Value Ease of Shopping.

One of the best things about ordering food at McDonald's is you know that no matter which restaurant you go to in the world, it's always going to be the same, easy experience: line up, tell the cashier which numbered meal you'd like, and then wait to be asked if you want to upsize it.

Unless your online store closely mimics the kind of experience shoppers have come to expect from marketplaces they'll get confused. And if they get confused, they'll go shop somewhere where they won't.

Of course, you can still maintain a unique brand on marketplaces like Etsy, Amazon and eBay, and you don't have to sacrifice individuality nearly as much as you think. Three ways you can do this are to bundle products and offer a better deal on them, sell brands that are truly new in the world, and find a marketplace that allows you to sell personalized items Amazon now fits the bill with its recently announced Amazon Brand Registry programmer.

Your online business no matter if you plan to make it your sole source of income or a side hobby deserves to get all the breaks it can. One of the easiest ways of establishing a solid foundation is to go with one of the tried-and-tested online marketplaces like Amazon, giving you much more leverage than you would tend to with your own store.

Benefit Of Becoming A Freelancer

If you are considering becoming a freelancer, or if you have been made redundant and are finding yourself pushed in this direction, there are a number of reasons why it could be a very good move. Now, we're not denying there are not a few downsides to freelancing (we promise there are only a few), but let's start with the nicer aspects of being your own boss. Whatever your industry sector, there are numerous advantages to be gained, so we thought it might help to give you the full list of pro's all in one place:

Financial Benefits:

The first thing that most people think of is the financial benefits, and these are of course very compelling. For example:

An average freelancer rate can easily be double or triple that of a full time employee, or even more.

Freelancers are paid higher rates due to the flexible nature of the relationship and the fact that many projects can be relatively short-term, although this isn't always the case, some contracts/assignments can last for years.

Depending on your individual skills and on the state of the industry in which you work (or the market in general) you can command very high rates of pay.

As a freelancer, you are paid for every hour that you work, as well as having the opportunity to work overtime at very good rates.

You can also work for multiple clients at the same time, on many different projects, which can also increase your pay.

If you take professional advice you can, as a freelancer, generally reduce your tax bill significantly.

Flexibility:

As a freelancer you are, in effect, your own boss - something which can be very satisfying and extremely enjoyable!

Freelancers have the ability to be far more independent than permanent employees.

You have the freedom to work when you choose, where you choose (depending on available projects of course) and for however long you like. There is a direct link between work effort and reward which sometimes doesn't exist as an employee.

Freelancers can take as much or as little holiday as they prefer you sign your own holiday form.

The companies you work for are not your employers, but are instead your clients, who put a whole different flavor on the relationship; you will be treated more as an equal and less as a member of staff.

Freelance projects will give you much more flexibility when it comes to agreeing conditions and terms.

As a freelancer you also have more flexibility over the payment terms that you can negotiate.

You have the opportunity to develop your career in a way that suits your personal circumstances at any given time.

Skills Development:

As a freelancer you will naturally work in different roles and for many different companies, and this will help you to build a unique range of skills and experience. Working as a freelancer gives you the opportunity to maybe test out other industry sectors to see if you can widen your experience.

Freelancers tend to gain a really good insight into different company cultures, processes, operations and structures.

Working in many different companies gives you the ability to build up a wide-ranging CV and to establish an extensive list of reference contacts.

A good freelancer will become known within their own field for their excellent work and you may even find that your services become sought-after, rather that you having to pitch for new projects or contracts all the time.

Carrying out project work in different organizations and environments gives a freelancer the opportunity to develop existing skills and to learn new ones.

As a freelancer you will be exposed to many different styles of working, not only in relation to your peers, but also in relation to your clients and your suppliers. This helps you to develop as an individual in more ways that just your core skill set.

Benefits of Network Marketing

- **I Don't Have To Stock or Ship Inventory**

This is also a massive expense for business owners and another one of the benefits of network marketing they may be interested in.

I love being able to tell entrepreneurs and business owners my inventory is stored in warehouses, no cost to me, and drop shipped at no cost to me, to the end consumer.

Any business owner that has to stock and ship their goods is going to love to hear this.

- **My Partnerships Don't Require Babysitting or Hand Holding.**

Another big headache business owners have with their brick and mortar shops is the fact that they have to be there 24/7.

And even if they aren't, they still have to deal with the #1 issue: employees benefits of multi level marketing.

Most business owners I know end up being at their location EVEN IF they have employees due to the fear or concern that the employee is going to mess up or steal something.

This makes this reason a huge draw for them when partnered with no need for hiring.

I love to say something along the lines of: "The biggest reason I love this profession is because I don't need to hire employees and the people I do partner with don't require my constant presence or hand-holding. I train them one time and then release them to perform their best."

Powerful stuff to a business owner.

Not so powerful when heard by an employee. Employees require a different form of communication that usually revolves around product or passive income.

- **There Are No Limitations on The Amount of Revenue You Can Generate**

So this is important in the way you say it. Benefits residual income using the word "revenue" will get any business owner to perk up.

And when you state one of the benefits of network marketing being the fact that no income ceiling exists you will definitely have their attention.

Most brick and mortar businesses can only reach a certain number of potential clients like I mentioned before, and the fact that this barrier is broken with the power of the internet is very incentivizing to anyone with a lick of entrepreneurship in them. Usually I say this: "The greatest draw I know concerning the benefits of network marketing is the ability to build a passive income stream with no limitations on how big you can go. Geographic boundaries are not a limitation doing what we do."

- **It Can Create Legacy Income**

Another one of the major benefits of network marketing is that this business can be passed on seamlessly to your children. It also takes little to no training to hand it off and if built correctly truly can become a passive income stream for them. The late and great Bill Britt built two successful Amway businesses in both North America and India, and was able to pass these on to his children who will reap the benefits of his hard work for years to come.

- **It Can Fulfill Life's Purpose**

Most business owners cannot say they are running the business they know they were meant to be running. I know too many successful businessmen and women that would leave their current business at the drop of a hat if the money were not a trap for them. In this profession when you stand in front of a business owner and tell them with 100% certainty you're doing what you're meant to be doing in business it stands out in a big way. Professionals listen to words when they're spoken from a position of certainty, authority, and with a sense of purpose.

Using these benefits of network marketing in your communication will 100% improve your results in sponsoring business owners? It's allowed us to bring on board six leaders that built either six or seven figure incomes in their previous companies.

Chapter 7
Tips for Starting a Profitable Company

How many business owners do you know that opened a business with the intention of that business failing? Hopefully that figure is low like zero percent low. But failure is often a part of starting a business, whether it's intentional or not. I have failed several times in my life, several of which were epic failures.

I've learned 20 different ways not to start a company. If you want to avoid failure as much as possible, then you need to learn from other people's mistakes. It' helps to start off with a bang. Starting a business correctly won't just help its chances of survival; it will also determine how profitable the business can be.

Here are a few things that I've learned along the way that will help you to starting a more profitable business.

- **Build a Strong Foundation**

Before you get too invested into your business idea, ask yourself why you're starting this venture in the first place. How is your product or service going to help your target audience better their lives? How does this idea align with your core values? Do you have a solid business plan to make this dream become a reality?

Answering questions like these will help ensure that your business has a strong foundation. From that starting point, you can continue to build a strong, reliable, and profitable business. While there will continue to be times when you have to adapt to changes in the market, you can always fall back on your strong foundation to help keep you in a straight line to success.

One of the strongest foundations I recommend that every entrepreneur has is to have a passion for what your'e doing. Be willing to work for years without being paid. Not saying you won't be paid, but I find when you have that foundation... you increase your chances for success significantly.

- **Surround Yourself With the Right People**

You've probably come across the phrase, "It takes a village to raise a child," at one point. Oddly enough, that quote can even be used to describe a successful business. Without the talented individuals working with you, do you honestly think that your business is going to survive? I personally like to surround myself with amazing friends and successful business owners.

Whether it's a co-founder, business partner, or team members that you hire as your business grows, these people possess different skills and knowledge that you may not have. When you team pulls their talent together, your business will be rounded out and able to thrive since it doesn't have any weak links.

Richard Branson has stated on the American Express Open Forum that the success of his Virgin businesses were due to building a great management team, "that had a vision, passion and a real sense of ownership," as well as being able to listen to feedback from employees and customers.

- **Know Your Enemies**

That may sound a bit harsh. But, your enemies are your competitors. While you're obviously not going to war with them, they are still a serious threat to your survival. However, that doesn't mean that you can't learn a thing or two from them - both good and bad. Remembering that you can learn as much from a poor or weak example as from a good one. For example, how have they been able to turn a profit? Have they made any social media blunders or mistakes?

Don't hesitate to analyze your top competitors with tools like SEMrush, Similar Web, or even just setting up a Google Alert to stay updated on any news regarding the competition.

- **Discover Ways to Keep Costs Low**

Positive cash flow is essential, but it isn't going to help much if you're just pouring money down the drain. That's why you need to be frugal as much as you can - as you build your business. For example, you can use free apps and software instead of purchasing software - no need for Microsoft Word when Google Docs work just fine.

You may also consider outsourcing some work instead of hiring full-time employees, renting out unused space in your office, renting or purchasing pre-owned equipment, or even splitting costs with another business - such as co-hosting an event together. Remember that there are 53+ million freelancers out there, that's a lot of people to help you create the company. When I started my company Due I had 14 different freelancers and only 2 full time people for the first 6 months. It's ok to use contractors; they can help you save money.

- **Embrace Creativity and Innovation**

Think about brands like Apple or IKEA. They've been able to stand the test of time and earn loyal followers because they succeeded at changing with the times, differentiated themselves from their competitors, and welcomed innovation. Despite what you think of either brand, both are very innovative and in very different verticals.

Don't dismiss new ideas from your team members or those which your customers share with you. Don't allow yourself to become afraid to use these new ideas and innovations and don't allow yourself to think that there's too much risk involved with new creative ideas. Try not to be worried that each new idea will cost too much. Offering new products or services or developing a clever marketing campaign not only gives you a competitive edge, being creative and innovative can help increase your profits as well.

- **Brand Yourself**

The name of your business has to get in front in the eyes of your audience. Whether it's networking in the industry, writing blog posts, guest contributing on leading industry publications, hosting a webinar or podcast, or interacting with your customers on social media, you have to promote yourself. It will not only spread brand awareness and increase your visibility - connecting with your audience will assist you in generating leads, which can convert into sales.

When you're establishing and promoting your brand, make sure that you are consistent across all channels and create high quality content that your audience will want to share. Go back to your core values and business plan if you need guidance on how you want your brand to be perceived.

- **Empower Your Staff**

Whether you have just one employee or fifty, you should always empower them by letting their voices be heard and contribute to business decisions. Be transparent with your team and applaud them for their successes - give them the freedom to work, and let them proudly announce that they're part of your team. When you have empowered employees, it creates passion and enthusiasm and of great importance, it creates energy that is easily picked up by customers.

- **Consistently Learn**

Have you already launched and managed a profitable company? If not - and don't take offense to this - you really don't know what it takes to start a successful company. Take the time to learn the fundamentals of starting a business. Learn skills that can make you more of an asset to your business. Stay on top of the latest industry trends. Work on strengthening your weaknesses.

Whether it's taking a class, reading an instructional book, finding a mentor, or hiring an expert, successful business owners are always looking to expand their knowledge and skill-set in order to better serve the business.

Chapter 8
Conclusion

From this book, I hope you realize the importance of evaluating a passive income opportunity. Make the right choice, don't waste time and leverage whenever you can. All of us have only 24 hours a day, so spend them wisely.

I have found the right Internet-based passive income opportunity. Competing in the $64 billion industry of personal development and having the right mentors and resources to guide me, I as well on the way to building a sustainable stream of passive income.

I am also actively looking for team members to take advantage of this passive income opportunity, making money online for a living is not difficult if you know where to get the right information, using the above information will allow you to work from anywhere and make a nice living.

Building multiple passive income streams is a great way to secure yourself for the future. You never know if you will be laid off from your regular job, get too ill to work, experience a disaster or want to start saving for your retirement.

Choose one of the above types of passive income streams and take action now, to secure your financial future…

ONE LAST THING...

If you enjoyed this book or found it useful I'd be very grateful if you'd post a short review on Amazon. Your support really does make a difference and I read all the reviews personally so I can get your feedback and make this book even better.

Thanks again for your support!

God bless you!!!

www.ingramcontent.com/pod-product-compliance
Lightning Source LLC
Chambersburg PA
CBHW050242230526
45470CB00005B/2078